DINOSAUR SCIENCE

WERE DINOSAURS JUST SHOW-OFFS?

BY DR. DAVE HONE AND DAVE SMITH

Enslow PUBLISHING

Published in 2026 by Enslow Publishing, LLC
2544 Clinton Street
Buffalo, NY 14224

First published in Great Britain in 2023 by Wayland

Editors: Christina Webb and Elise Short
Design: Emma DeBanks

Printed in China

CPSIA compliance information: Batch #QW26ENS: For further information contact Enslow Publishing LLC, New York, New York at 1-800-398-2504.

Please visit our website, www.enslowpublishing.com. For a free color catalog of all our high-quality books, call toll free 1-800-398-2504 or fax 1-877-980-4454.

Cataloging-in-Publication Data
Names: Hone, David (Paleontologist), author. | Smith, Dave, illustrator.
Title: Were dinosaurs just show-offs? / by Dr. Dave Hone, illustrated by Dave Smith.
Description: Buffalo, NY : Enslow Publishing, 2026. |
Series: Dinosaur science | Includes glossary and index.
Identifiers: ISBN 9781978547223 (pbk.) | ISBN 9781978547230 (library bound) | ISBN 9781978547247 (ebook)
Subjects: LCSH: Dinosaurs--Juvenile literature. | Dinosaurs--Behavior--Juvenile literature. | Extinct reptiles--Juvenile literature. | Paleontology--Juvenile literature.
Classification: LCC QE862.D5 H66 2026 | DDC 567.9--dc23

CONTENTS

LOTS OF DIFFERENT DINOSAURS

Animal bodies and behaviors sometimes change over time so they can do something better or different. This is called adaptation and evolution. It happens in response to the ever-changing conditions around them. If there are large predators (hunters) about, an animal might develop longer legs to run away faster, better eyesight to see the predator coming, or armor to fend them off.

Dinosaurs Everywhere

Dinosaurs were around for over 150 million years and lived on every continent and in every environment, from rainforests to coasts to deserts. Across the 1,500 species that paleontologists have named so far, there is a huge variety in each of their bodies – from hands and feet, to teeth and jaws, to tails and ribs.

Evolution had a lot of time and a lot of dinosaurs to play with! Read on to find out about some of the most amazing parts of different dinosaur bodies.

SIGHTS AND SOUNDS

Good eyesight and hearing is important for herbivores (plant eaters) to make sure they know if any carnivores (meat eaters) are coming, and carnivores need good eyesight and hearing to find prey (the animals they hunt).

Look Out!

The legendary carnivore *Tyrannosaurus* is famous for its tiny arms. But it also had some of the biggest eyes of any land animal ever to have lived. They could be as large as a tennis ball! This meant that it was good at seeing things a very long way away and could see well in the dark too. If you were prey, standing still in the dark would not keep you safe!

Ear, Ear

A group of small, feathered dinosaurs called troodontids had big eyes too, but some also had very odd ears – one was higher up than the other. This feature meant that they could identify exactly how far a sound was. This is something we also see in today's small, feathered predators – owls!

Paleontologists think that troodontids' amazing eyes and ears helped them hunt small animals in the dark.

REACHING UP AND OUT

If you are a herbivore, food can be a long way away. It might be up high in a tree, or deep into a thicket, but the good news is, a long neck should help you reach it. Also, if you are very big and heavy, moving is a lot of effort so a long neck can help you grab more food without having to shift your bulk.

Long Necks And Tiny Heads

The sauropod dinosaurs are famous for their long necks and tiny heads. The necks were light because the bones were hollow (empty), and, combined with a small head, it was easy for a sauropod to move around and grab as much food as possible.

How Long?

Some sauropods had really long parts on their neck bones which overlapped and fit together perfectly to help hold their necks up. The longest neck belonged to a Chinese sauropod called *Mamenchisaurus*. It was 43 feet (13 m) long, half the length of its full body – imagine what you would look like if you were half neck!

GETTING AROUND

Dinosaurs had a wide variety of features and adaptations to help them move around.

Gripping Toes

Some moved on two legs and others on all fours, but they all had toes that splayed out with claws on them to help them grip the ground.

The fastest dinosaurs, including the ornithomimosaurs, looked and acted a lot like ostriches. They were lightly built with very long legs.

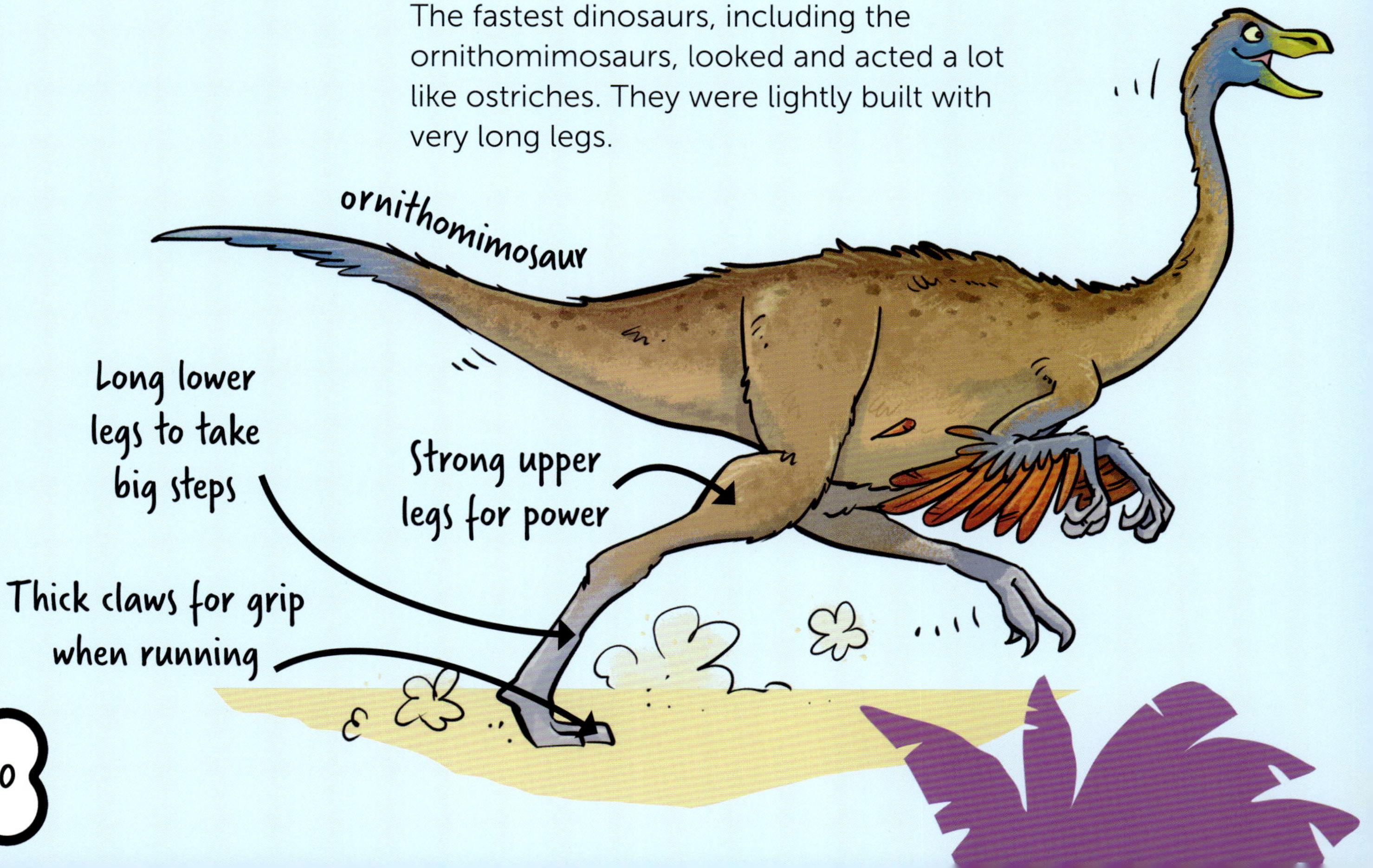

DID YOU KNOW?

Not all dinosaurs were running around on the ground. Several groups of small-feathered dinosaurs lived in and around trees and were able to glide from branch to branch. Many of these had wings, but some had bizarre bat-like wings and feathers too.

Funny Toe Bones

The ornithomimosaurs and several other dinosaurs had an odd pattern of bones in their feet where they were squeezed together. This stopped them from jiggling around when they ran – it took less energy for them to run than other dinosaurs.

TALES OF TAILS

The long tails of dinosaurs had lots of uses.

Staying Up

For those that walked on two legs, the tail was an important counterbalance to keep them up, but for all dinosaurs the tail was essential to help them move.

The Tail End

Dinosaurs had a very large block of muscles that attached the tail to the back of their thigh bones. When the tail muscles pulled the leg backward, it pushed the animal forward. This means that a dinosaur's tail did most of the work for walking and running.

Smash!

Tails could be useful in other ways, too. Lots of the ankylosaurs (armored dinosaurs) had a club at the end of their tail which they used to fight off predators or even each other. Dinosaur tails were great for fighting and running away!

PLANT EATERS' JAWS AND TEETH

Animals that eat plants often need to eat a lot of them. This is because leaves are not very nutritious.

Dino Hoover

The sauropod *Nigersaurus* was unusual in having a short neck, but even stranger was its very wide vacuum-cleaner mouth. Its wide jaws allowed it to chop off more leaves per bite than small-mouthed herbivores and eat faster than its competitors.

More Leaves Please!

Most plant-eating dinosaurs are from a group called the ornithischians. These animals had a beak at the front of their mouths and teeth to chop or grind up their food in the back. This was useful for slicing off parts of tough plants before eating them.

DID YOU KNOW?

Some beaked plant-eating theropods, such as *Sinornithomimus*, didn't have any teeth but swallowed small stones which helped grind up food in the stomach (ducks and chickens do something similar today). These can be found in some fossils and are called gastroliths meaning "stomach stones." Sounds painful!

MEAT EATERS' TEETH

There were many types of meat-eating dinosaur and they had a wide variety of adaptations to catch and eat their prey. Often they had different-shaped teeth to do different jobs.

Teeth Like Saws

Most theropods such as *Allosaurus* had thin, curved sawlike teeth. This made them incredibly sharp and very good at cutting through meat.

Spiky Teeth

One group of theropods called the spinosaurs ate a lot of fish. They had simple teeth that were like a row of cone-shaped spikes just like we see in crocodiles and dolphins. Spikes like this are great for holding onto small slippery foods like fish.

DID YOU KNOW?

Tyrannosaurus and its relatives had two types of teeth in their jaws. At the sides, they had thick and strong teeth that could break up bones. At the front, they had some short teeth pressed together that were great at scraping the meat from bones. They had teeth for every job!

CLEVER CLAWS

Claws were not just used to help dinosaurs grip when they ran or climbed, but they were adapted for various uses in different dinosaurs.

Claws For Catching

Many theropods had sharp claws on their hands that would have helped them catch their prey. Other dinosaurs had more unusual claws.

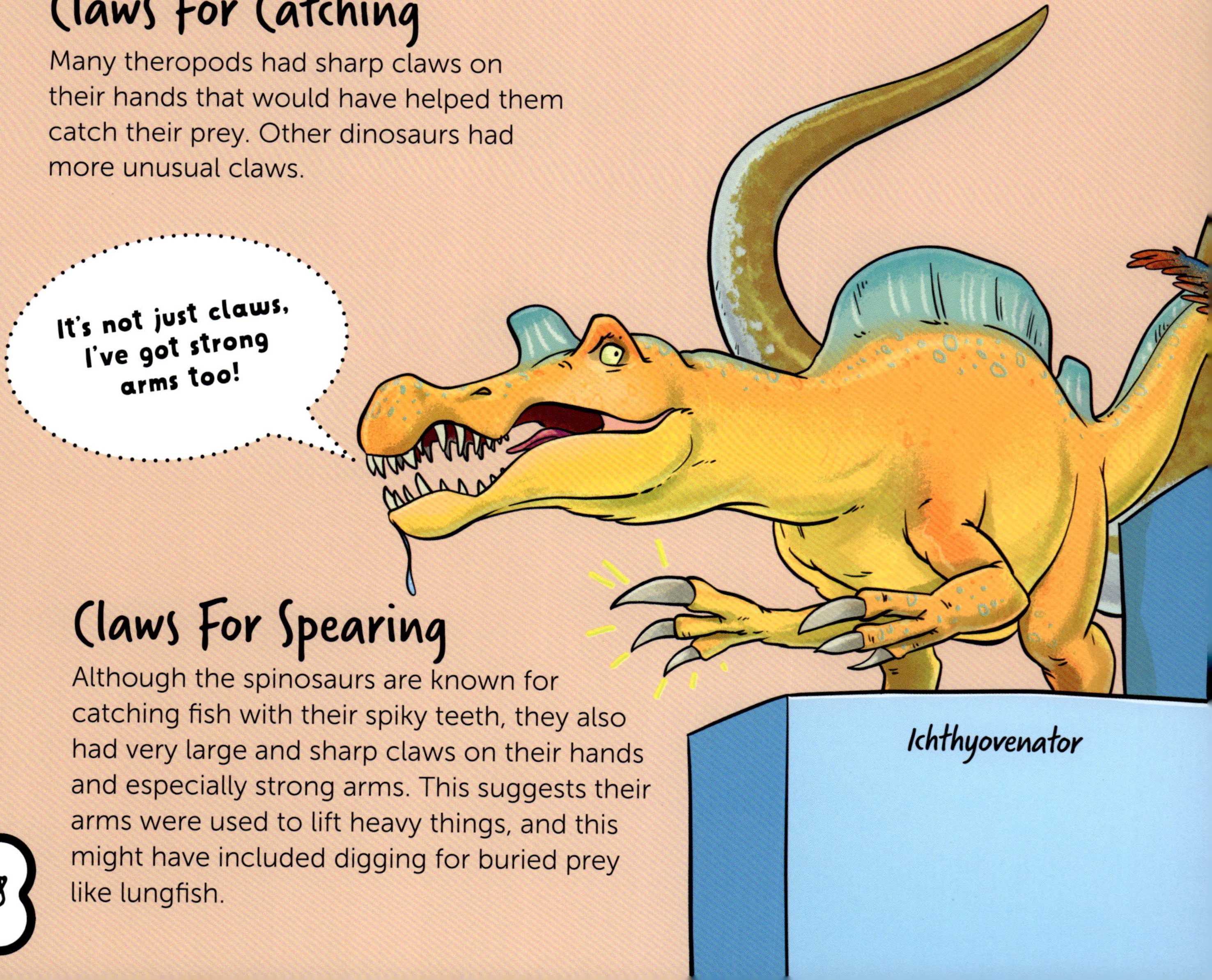

Claws For Spearing

Although the spinosaurs are known for catching fish with their spiky teeth, they also had very large and sharp claws on their hands and especially strong arms. This suggests their arms were used to lift heavy things, and this might have included digging for buried prey like lungfish.

DID YOU KNOW?

Claws aren't just for hunting! Some of the biggest sauropods – plant eaters – had large, strong claws on their front feet that would have been very useful for digging nests to lay their eggs.

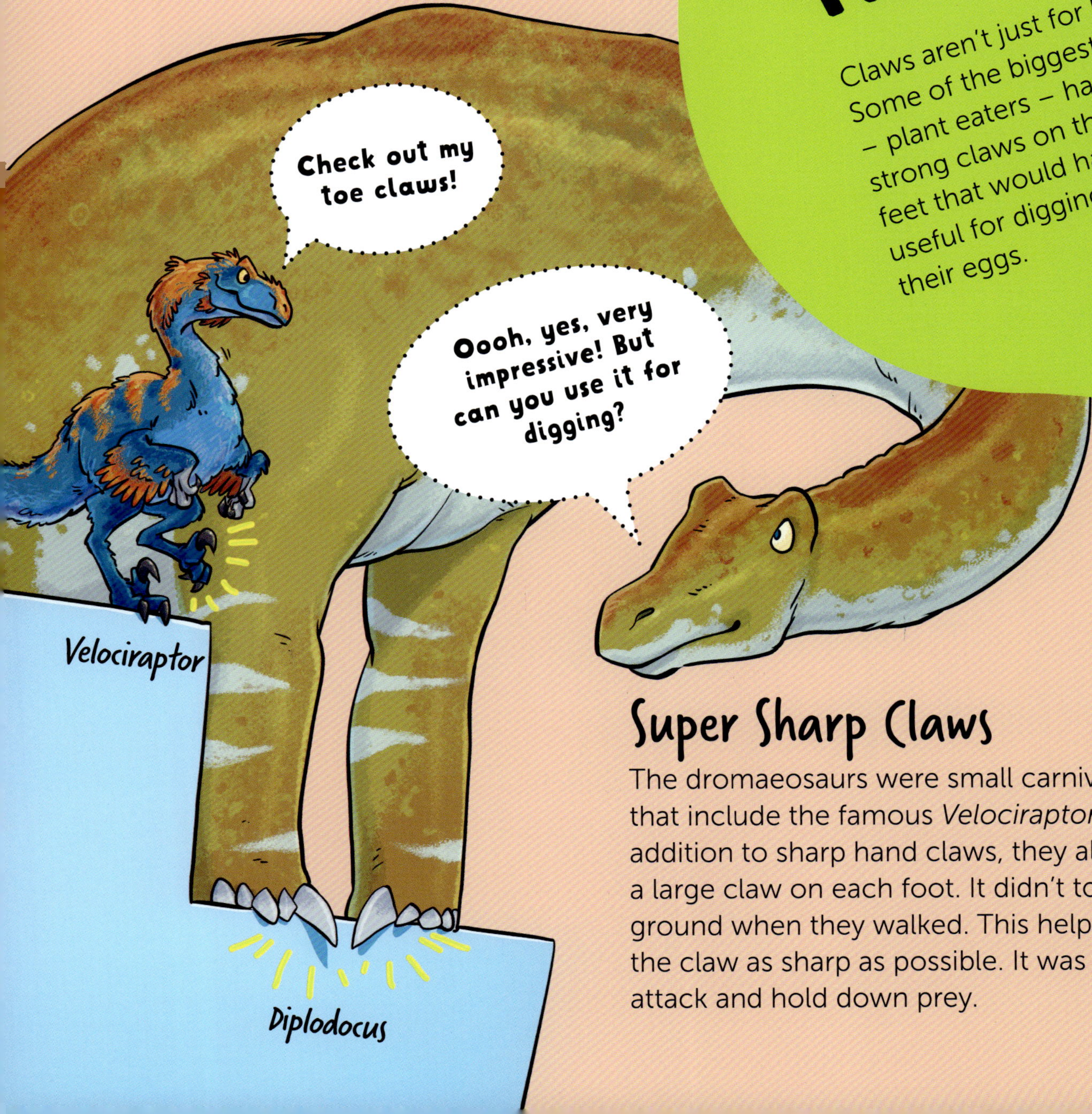

Super Sharp Claws

The dromaeosaurs were small carnivores, that include the famous *Velociraptor*. In addition to sharp hand claws, they also had a large claw on each foot. It didn't touch the ground when they walked. This helped keep the claw as sharp as possible. It was used to attack and hold down prey.

DINOSAUR FIGHTS

Carnivores tried to kill other dinosaurs in order to eat them, but dinosaurs would fight each other for other reasons too. They had all sorts of weapons: sharp fangs, pointy claws, horns, spikes, and bumps to attack one another.

Body Weapons

Meat-eating theropods had sharp teeth and claws for fighting and hunting. Many plant-eating ornithischians also evolved weapons, used to fight other dinosaurs.

Ceratopsians, such as *Triceratops,* had a wide variety of horns, spikes, and bumps on their heads. Paleontologists (dinosaur scientists) have found fossil skeletons of *Triceratops* with healed wounds where the horns of their opponents hit them during a fight.

What A Bone Head!

The name *Pachycephalosaurus* means "thick-headed reptile." These animals had extremely thick skulls and would ram into each other to try and knock over or injure their opponents!

Small But Mighty

Even the smallest of dinosaurs fought sometimes. The little heterodontosaurs were often only 2 feet (0.6 m) long, but these herbivores had long sharp fangs in their jaws that could be used to bite one another.

KEEPING SAFE

Several different dinosaur groups evolved to defend themselves with the protection of armor.

Armor All Over

Ankylosaurs were too slow to run away from attackers. But they had a way of protecting themselves from danger! They had a huge number of spikes and lumps of bone and the top and sides of their body were almost completely covered in armor. It was so extreme they even had chunks of bone on their eyelids to protect their eyes!

DID YOU KNOW?

Other dinosaurs had armor too, including some of the long-necked sauropods. *Saltasaurus* from South America also had rows of bony armor to help protect it from large theropods.

Spiky Stegosaurs

The stegosaurs also had various plates and spikes along their backs and often had giant shoulder spines to protect their sides.

SHOWING OFF: THE HERBIVORES

Living in the dinosaurs' world was not always about being eaten or fighting. Lots of dinosaurs had body adaptations that helped them find a partner.

How Do I Look?

Dinosaurs had a range of crests and frills to show how good they looked. Ceratopsians did this well. In addition to their horns, they also had a big frill around the back of their head that acted as a giant sign.

Musical Heads

Lots of dinosaurs had all kinds of fancy headgear to show off. Many of the hadrosaurs had big bony growths on their heads. For some, these growths would also have helped them make loud noises to attract attention too.

DID YOU KNOW?

The spinosaurs (them again, see pages 17 and 18) had a fin-like tail and a giant sail along their backs that they used to show off. And they weren't the only ones – a large ornithischian from Africa called *Ouranosaurus* had a huge sail too.

SHOWING OFF: THE CARNIVORES

Lots of theropods had bony head crests, but those that evolved later had another trick: feathers. Like their descendants – birds – many feathered theropods had long feathers with which they could show off!

Beautiful Plumage

Incredibly, for a few of these feathery dinosaurs, traces of the original colors remain in the fossils. So we know that some had brightly colored feathers. We've even found a dinosaur with iridescent rainbow-like plumage, known as *Caihong juji!*

Flaunting Fans

Perhaps the best example is a group of dinosaurs from Asia and North America called the oviraptorosaurs. Many of the best-preserved ones show a fan of feathers on the end of their tails rather like a peacock (though smaller). Even better, fossils show that they had bones that enabled them to flap their tail up and down to show off their fans.

WHAT NEXT?

For the last ten years, paleontologists have named a new dinosaur nearly every week – that's almost 500 new species! We keep finding ever more interesting and more unusual dinosaurs, as well as new and interesting parts of old ones. Here are a few of the most interesting finds from recent years.

Deinocheirus

For years, this huge dinosaur was known only by a pair of long arms. We now know it had a big head and a hump on its back and may have eaten fish.

Stegorous

A small relative of stegosaurs and ankylosaurs, *Stegorous* had a tail with some sharp blade-like bones on the sides giving it an axe-like attack.

Balaur

Originally thought to be a dromaeosaur, this carnivore had a pair of giant claws on each foot rather than just one. More recent studies suggest it might have been an early flightless bird!

It Could Be You!

Who knows what else we might find next? And if you become a paleontologist one day, what do you think you might discover?

GLOSSARY

Adaption – a feature on an animal that works well to do something different or better than it did in the ancestors of that animal.

Carnivore – an animal that mostly or entirely eats meat – this can include things like fish and insects as well as land animals.

Counterbalance – to balance out another weight.

Dinosaur – a group of extinct reptiles that were the dominant land animals from around 225–65 million years ago. Their descendants live on today as birds.

Evolution – the natural process where over time species of organisms change in response to their environment.

Fossil – the remains of an ancient animal or plant (or remains from their movements, like footprints) that have turned to stone.

Gliding – a form of flying that doesn't involve any flapping. Gliding animals lose height as they move so end up below where they started and need to climb to fly again.

Herbivore – an animal that mostly or entirely eats plants including leaves, seeds, fruit, and even wood.

Ornithischian – a group of plant-eating dinosaurs. Some walked on two legs and others on four, and many of them had armor or head crests with spikes on them.

Paleontologist – a scientist who studies ancient life. Not just dinosaurs, but also other animals, plants, and ancient environments.

Sauropod – a group of large dinosaurs with long necks and tails. All of them walked on four legs and ate plants.

Theropod – a group of meat-eating dinosaurs (though some switched and ate plants) that walked on two legs.

FURTHER INFORMATION

Books

Body Bits: Dead-awesome Dinosaur Body Facts by Paul Mason and Dave Smith (Wayland, 2021)

Dinosaur Infosaurus series by Katie Woolley (Wayland, 2021)

Dino-Sorted series by Sonya Newland and Izzi Howell (Gareth Stevens Publishing, 2026)

Websites

Find out about dinosaurs and prehistoric life:
kids.nationalgeographic.com/animals/prehistoric

Watch a video explaining how we know what color dinosaurs were:
youtu.be/qYijAZWdnBk

Explore the Natural History Museum's directory of dinosaurs:
www.nhm.ac.uk/discover/dino-directory.html

Play games, watch videos, and learn about paleontology:
www.amnh.org/explore/ology/paleontology

INDEX